T0395026

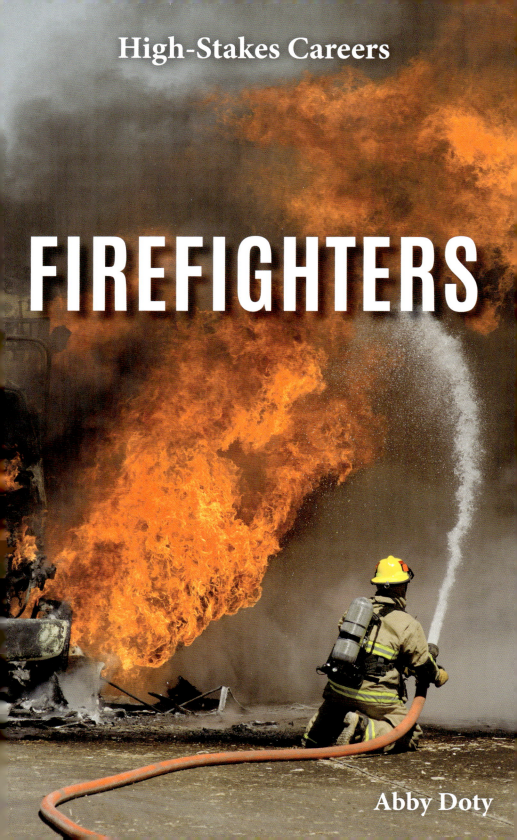

High-Stakes Careers

FIREFIGHTERS

Abby Doty

Apex is distributed by North Star Editions:
sales@northstareditions.com | 888-417-0195

Produced for Apex by Red Line Editorial.

Photographs ©: Shutterstock Images, cover, 1, 6–7, 10–11, 16–17, 18–19, 26–27, 28–29, 30–31, 32–33, 36–37, 40–41, 42–43, 44–45, 46–47, 49, 50–51, 52–53; UPI/Bettmann Archive/Getty Images, 4–5; iStockphoto, 8–9, 12–13, 14–15, 24–25, 34–35, 54–55, 56–57, 58; Paul Harris/Archive Photos/Getty Images, 20–21; Alex Brandon/AP Images, 22–23; Rick Diamond/Getty Images News/Getty Images, 39

Library of Congress Control Number: 2025930914

ISBN
979-8-89250-671-7 (hardcover)
979-8-89250-705-9 (ebook pdf)
979-8-89250-689-2 (hosted ebook)

Printed in the United States of America
Mankato, MN
082025

NOTE TO PARENTS AND EDUCATORS

Apex books are designed to build literacy skills in striving readers. Exciting, high-interest content attracts and holds readers' attention. The text is carefully leveled to allow students to achieve success quickly.

TABLE OF CONTENTS

Chapter 1

JUST IN TIME

In August 1972, a fire tore through an apartment building in Chicago, Illinois. Several floors began to collapse. Some firefighters ran inside to save people. Others climbed ladders to rescue people from higher floors.

Chicago firefighters often fight more than 1,000 structure fires each year.

STAY BACK
500 FT.

CHICA

One woman yelled that her son was still on the fifth floor. Firefighters ran through smoke and flames to search for him. One firefighter found the boy and carried him. The fifth floor collapsed as the firefighters ran. But they and the boy escaped. The boy's mother ran to hug them.

FAST FIRE

The fire started small. It began on the fifth floor. But it spread very quickly. Firefighters were just a few minutes away. By the time they arrived, all seven floors were burning. About 100 people had to evacuate.

Firefighters may shine lights to see through smoke in burning buildings.

More than one million people in the United States work as firefighters.

Chapter 2

WHAT FIREFIGHTERS DO

Firefighters help in emergencies. They are best known for putting out fires. But they also respond to other types of calls. They rush to places where people need help or rescue.

Many firefighters work at fire stations. Each station is in charge of a certain area. When there's a problem, the station gets a call from emergency services. The call tells firefighters where and what the issue is. The firefighters quickly get ready. They grab gear and drive off in a fire truck. They race to the scene with their lights and sirens on.

FULL-TIME OR PART-TIME

Some people work as firefighters full-time. A shift typically lasts 24 hours. During it, firefighters live at the fire station. Between shifts, they often get 48 hours off. Other firefighters are volunteers. They live near the station. They rush there to help during calls.

Dispatchers are people who answer emergency calls and send help. They usually alert the nearest fire station.

Firefighters are often the first people to arrive at an emergency. They start helping right away. For example, people may need medical care. Firefighters can help them until EMTs arrive. And some firefighters are trained to be EMTs, too.

HELPING AMBULANCES

Ambulances and fire trucks are both called for many medical emergencies. They often show up together. Many ambulances carry only two workers. Firefighters may help them treat hurt people. In some cases, fire trucks reach scenes first. Fire stations may be closer than hospitals.

Most fire trucks carry about four firefighters.

13

If there is a fire, firefighters work to put it out. They often use large hoses to spray water. The hoses connect to fire trucks or hydrants. They pour huge amounts of water onto the fire.

Firefighters may also use fire extinguishers. These tools spray chemicals or powder onto the fire to smother it.

FIGHTING THE FLAMES

One type of extinguisher is shaped like a ball. Firefighters throw it at a fire. When flames touch it, the ball explodes. It releases powder. This type of extinguisher works well for spaces that are small or hard to reach.

Some fire trucks can hold 1,000 gallons (3,785 L) of water.

Some fire truck ladders stretch more than 100 feet (30 m).

Firefighters also work to get people out of burning buildings. They rescue people who are trapped or hurt. They may use ladders to reach high floors. They may use axes to break down walls or doors. Firefighters may even run through flames to find people and carry them out.

A hazmat suit may cover a person's whole body. It may also provide air for them to breathe.

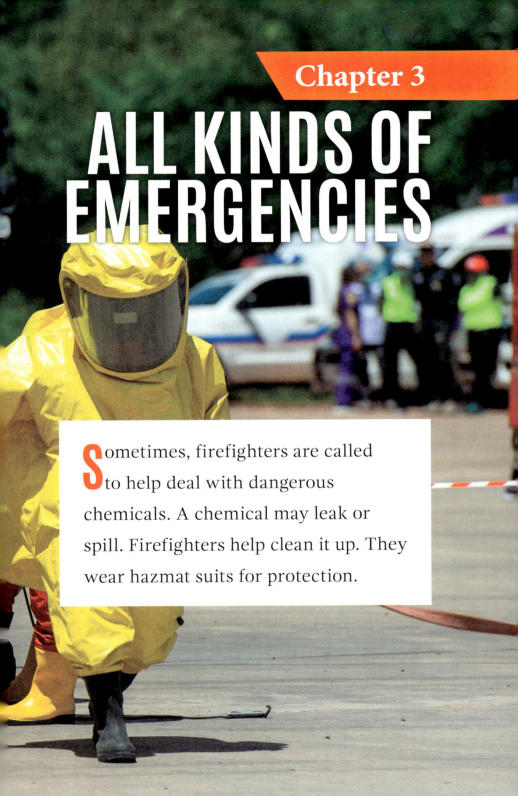

Chapter 3

ALL KINDS OF EMERGENCIES

Sometimes, firefighters are called to help deal with dangerous chemicals. A chemical may leak or spill. Firefighters help clean it up. They wear hazmat suits for protection.

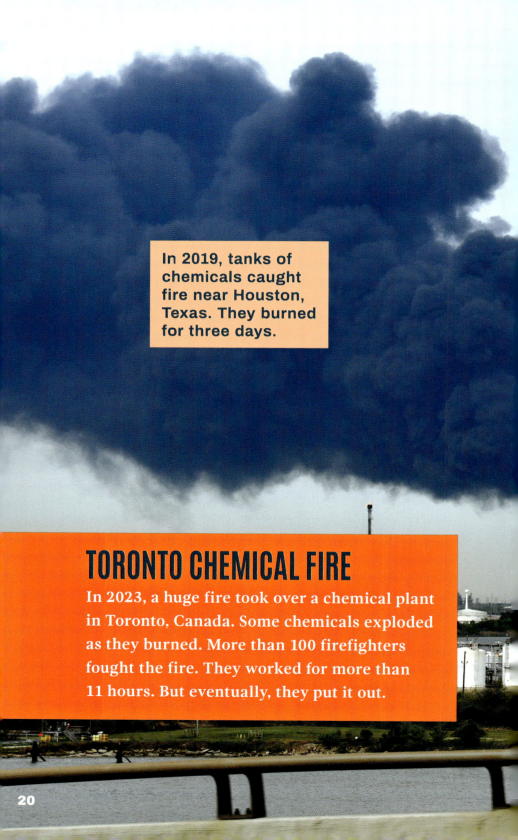

In 2019, tanks of chemicals caught fire near Houston, Texas. They burned for three days.

TORONTO CHEMICAL FIRE

In 2023, a huge fire took over a chemical plant in Toronto, Canada. Some chemicals exploded as they burned. More than 100 firefighters fought the fire. They worked for more than 11 hours. But eventually, they put it out.

Firefighters try to clean up chemicals as quickly as possible. That helps limit harm to nearby people or land. But this work is risky. Some chemicals catch fire very easily. They may even explode.

Chemical fires can be tricky to put out. Water often makes them worse. So, firefighters use other methods instead. For example, they may spray foam to smother the flames.

Firefighters also help after natural disasters. Examples include hurricanes, earthquakes, and tornadoes. These events cause massive damage. People may be stranded in flooded areas. Or they may be trapped beneath debris. Firefighters work to find and rescue them.

In 2005, Hurricane Katrina flooded much of New Orleans, Louisiana. Fire crews searched ruined buildings for people.

Firefighters may use ropes and stretchers to move injured people.

In fact, firefighters do many types of rescue work. Some involve people who are trapped in tight spaces. Examples include mines, elevators, and wells. Firefighters may use ropes to reach people. Or they may dig a new way out. But they must work quickly. Trapped people may be hurt. And if a rescue takes too long, they can run out of air.

CHILEAN MINE RESCUE

In 2010, a mine in Chile collapsed. A group of 33 miners became trapped 2,300 feet (700 m) below ground. They stayed there for months. Firefighters and other rescuers drilled a new tunnel. Then they pulled the miners up and out in a metal tube.

Sometimes, firefighters do all of these jobs at once. For example, in a car accident, vehicles may catch on fire. Firefighters put these fires out. If gas leaks, firefighters clean it up. That way, fires are less likely to start or spread. Firefighters also help people who are hurt or trapped by the crash.

JAWS OF LIFE

In some crashes, car doors are smashed shut. People may still be inside. To get them out, firefighters often use tools known as the Jaws of Life. The tools can bend and cut through metal. They help firefighters create openings.

With the Jaws of Life, firefighters can remove a car's roof in just a couple of minutes.

Large stations can send out many fire trucks.
Smaller stations may have just one truck.

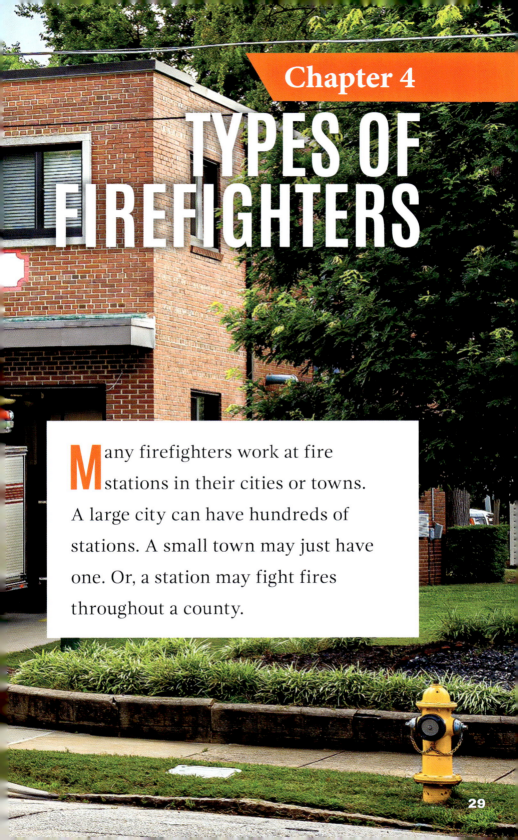

Chapter 4

TYPES OF FIREFIGHTERS

Many firefighters work at fire stations in their cities or towns. A large city can have hundreds of stations. A small town may just have one. Or, a station may fight fires throughout a county.

Other firefighters focus on wildfires. These fires burn in natural areas, such as forests and grasslands. They often start in remote places. Firefighters may have to make long journeys to reach them. They may walk or drive over rough land.

A BIG ISSUE

Wildfires spread quickly. They can travel 14 miles per hour (23 km/h). And they can stretch for miles. The huge flames burn everything they touch. Bad fires can destroy millions of acres of land.

Firefighters may watch for wildfires from tall lookout towers.

Bringing large fire trucks to remote areas is often too difficult. So, wildland firefighters use other methods. Firebreaks are one example. Fires need fuel to keep burning. So, firefighters dig to form a line of dirt. The fire can't spread past it. Firefighters may also use planes or helicopters. They drop chemicals or water on the flames.

IN THE WILDERNESS

Wildfires can take weeks or months to put out. Firefighters often live in the wilderness while they work. Each crew stays for two weeks. Then a new crew takes their place.

Helicopters carry water in huge buckets. Each bucket often holds 180 gallons (680 L) or more.

Some wildland firefighters train to be smoke jumpers. They jump from airplanes or helicopters. Then they parachute down to the ground. They land near wildfires. They try to bring the fires under control.

Other firefighters join hotshot crews. These crews fight the biggest and riskiest wildfires. They go right to the hottest, most dangerous parts.

ALASKAN WILDFIRE

In 2019, eight smoke jumpers fought a fire in Alaska. The fire burned more than 36,000 acres (14,570 ha). The smoke jumpers fought for 16 days. Flames nearly trapped them. But they managed to save nearby buildings.

The United States has more than 100 hotshot crews. They often use axes and shovels to fight fires.

Other firefighters specialize, too. Some focus on fighting industrial fires. They work at factories or warehouses. Others work at airports. They put out fires and rescue people who are hurt or in danger. But they also help with airplane crashes. And they clean up fuel spills.

Firefighters also serve in the military. They can respond to nearby accidents or wildfires. And they help during attacks. They stop fires on planes and ships. They care for injured soldiers, too.

Airport fire trucks are bigger and faster than fire trucks that drive on city streets. They also hold more water.

YARNELL HILL FIRE

In 2013, a lightning strike started a wildfire near Yarnell, Arizona. The huge fire burned more than 8,300 acres (3,360 ha). The Granite Mountain Hotshots tried to stop it. But the fire was too strong. Wind blew the fire toward them. The hotshots tried to hide in their fire shelters. These bags cover people to protect them from heat. But this fire reached 2,000 degrees Fahrenheit (1,093°C). Nineteen of the 20 hotshots died.

People set up memorials to honor the hotshots who fought the Yarnell Hill Fire.

Chapter 5

RISKS

Vehicle fires are especially dangerous. If fuel tanks catch fire, they can explode.

Firefighters face many dangers. Fires can cause terrible burns. Firefighters wear thick suits and gloves for protection. But some fires get hot enough to burn through them.

Air tanks may weigh 30 pounds (14 kg) or more.

Fires can make buildings unstable. Walls and ceilings may collapse. Firefighters can be crushed. Or they may fall while climbing roofs or ladders.

A fire's smoke is dangerous, too. Breathing smoke can make people pass out. It also harms their hearts and lungs. Firefighters often wear masks and carry air tanks. That way, they have clean air to breathe.

Even so, firefighters may still be exposed to dangerous chemicals. Some chemicals are in smoke. Others are in things that firefighters touch while cleaning up. Being around these chemicals can make people sick. It can even cause cancer. Firefighters are more likely to get that disease.

HARMFUL CHEMICALS

Some chemicals burn people's skin. Others cause damage when they get in people's eyes or lungs. Safety gear protects firefighters somewhat. But some chemicals still get into their bodies. This increases their risk for heart and lung problems.

Fire smoke contains carbon monoxide. Breathing this chemical can be deadly.

Wildland firefighters face even more challenges. They often work far from cities and towns. They must bring their supplies with them. They can use radios to call for help. But help may take a long time to arrive. By then, it may be too late.

Wildfires often burn in places with few roads. Getting near them can be a challenge. So can getting away.

FAILED JUMPS

Smoke jumping is very risky. Parachutes help slow people's falls. But sometimes, a parachute doesn't open. Smoke jumpers carry a second parachute in case this happens. But they can still get hurt. If they hit the ground too hard, they can break bones or even die.

9/11 FIREFIGHTERS

On September 11, 2001, terrorists flew planes into the World Trade Center in New York. The tall buildings caught on fire. Hundreds of firefighters ran to help. They couldn't stop the fire. So, they tried saving the people in the buildings. They got thousands of people out. Then the buildings collapsed. Dust and debris covered the city's streets. A total of 343 firefighters died that day. Hundreds more got sick later on. Many died from diseases caused by the fire.

During 9/11, firefighters saved more than 25,000 people.

Chapter 6

BECOMING A FIREFIGHTER

To become firefighters, people must finish high school. Some also go to college. They often get degrees in fire science. They learn common causes of fires and ways to prevent them.

The amount of time it takes to become a firefighter varies. Some people study and train for years. Others go through shorter programs.

Firefighters lift weights to prepare for carrying heavy gear.

Next, people apply to a firefighter training program. Getting in can be hard. People must pass physical tests. They must be fast and strong. They may also need to live near a fire station.

Most programs last a few weeks or months. Students learn how to bring different kinds of fires under control. For example, firefighters don't spray water on oil fires. Water can spread the oil and make the fire grow.

PRACTICE FIRES

To help students practice, trainers set empty buildings on fire. They have students work to put them out. They teach students how to use different tools and techniques. This gets students ready to fight real fires.

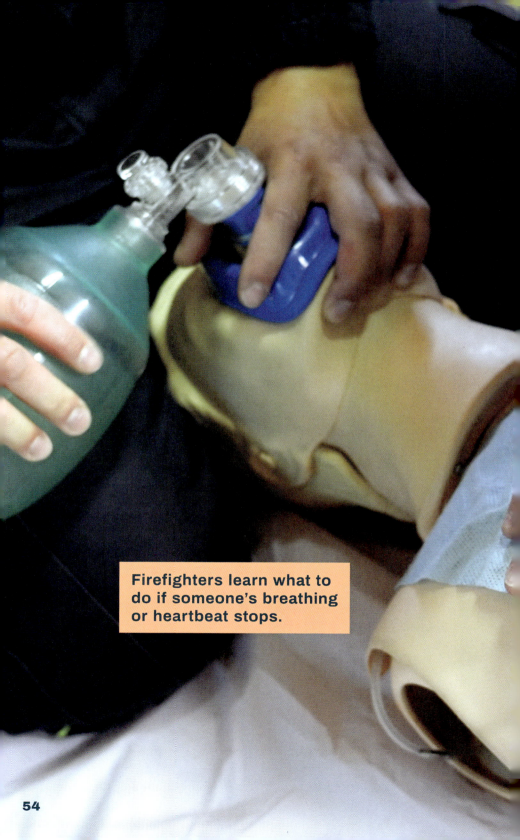

Firefighters learn what to do if someone's breathing or heartbeat stops.

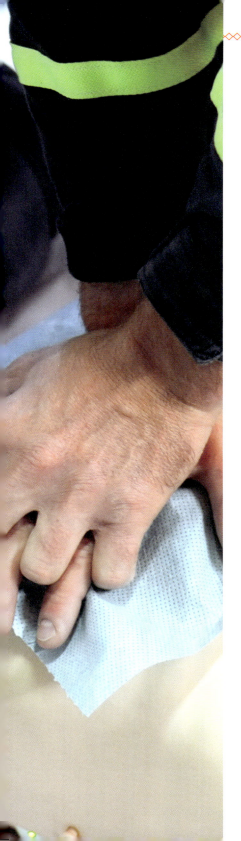

Students learn ways to keep fires from spreading. They practice rescuing people. They also learn CPR and first aid.

Students show these skills during a test at the program's end. If they pass, they are certified. They can get jobs.

Many jobs begin with a probation period. It usually lasts a few months. During this time, new firefighters keep learning and training. They build skills and experience.

Specialized firefighters go through even more training. Wildland firefighters study how wind and drought shape where fires will likely start and spread. And smoke jumpers learn how to use parachutes. These jobs often require a few years of experience. That prepares people for the added challenge.

VOLUNTEERS

Volunteer firefighters also need training. But not all get certified. Some go through shorter trainings. Local departments often run these.

Firefighters in Germany practice putting out a fire on a fake plane as part of their training to work at an airport.

✓ SKILLS CHECKLIST

- Giving basic first aid

- Lifting and carrying heavy equipment

- Staying calm in dangerous situations

- Thinking quickly under pressure

- Understanding fire science

- Working well in teams

COMPREHENSION QUESTIONS

Write your answers on a separate piece of paper.

1. Write a paragraph that explains the main ideas in Chapter 2.

2. Which type of firefighter do you think has the most interesting job? Why?

3. What type of work do hotshots do?
   - A. fight fires that burn factories
   - B. fight the biggest, riskiest wildfires
   - C. parachute down to fight wildfires

4. What would be a good method for fighting an oil fire?
   - A. spraying it with water from a hose
   - B. spraying it with a fire extinguisher
   - C. letting it burn

5. What does **unstable** mean in this book?

*Fires can make buildings **unstable**. Walls and ceilings may collapse.*

    A. likely to fall down
    B. likely to stay up
    C. likely to get bigger

6. What does **physical** mean in this book?

*People must pass **physical** tests. They must be fast and strong.*

    A. using ideas from the past
    B. relating to the mind
    C. relating to the body

Answer key on page 64.

GLOSSARY

county
One of several smaller areas that states are broken up into.

CPR
A treatment that can save a person whose heartbeat or breathing has stopped.

debris
Pieces of something that broke or fell apart.

drought
A time of little or no rain.

EMTs
People who are trained to give medical care during an emergency.

fire extinguishers
Tools that shoot water, foam, or gas to put out fires.

hazmat suits
Suits that keep out harmful chemicals.

hydrants
Large pipes that firefighters can attach hoses to and get water from.

industrial
Involving factories or other buildings where companies make or build products.

remote
Far away from towns or people.

terrorists
People who attack and scare others to reach their goals.

TO LEARN MORE

BOOKS

Dolbear, Emily. *Firefighters on the Scene.* The Child's World, 2022.

Hamilton, S. L. *Fire & Rescue Aircraft.* Abdo Publishing, 2022.

Reeves, Diane Lindsey. *What Firefighters Need to Know.* Cherry Lake Publishing, 2024.

ONLINE RESOURCES

Visit **www.apexeditions.com** to find links and resources related to this title.

ABOUT THE AUTHOR

Abby Doty is a writer, editor, and booklover from Minnesota.

INDEX

ANSWER KEY:
1. Answers will vary; 2. Answers will vary; 3. B; 4. B; 5. A; 6. C